GREAT WHITE SHARK

GIANTS AMONG US

Jason Cooper

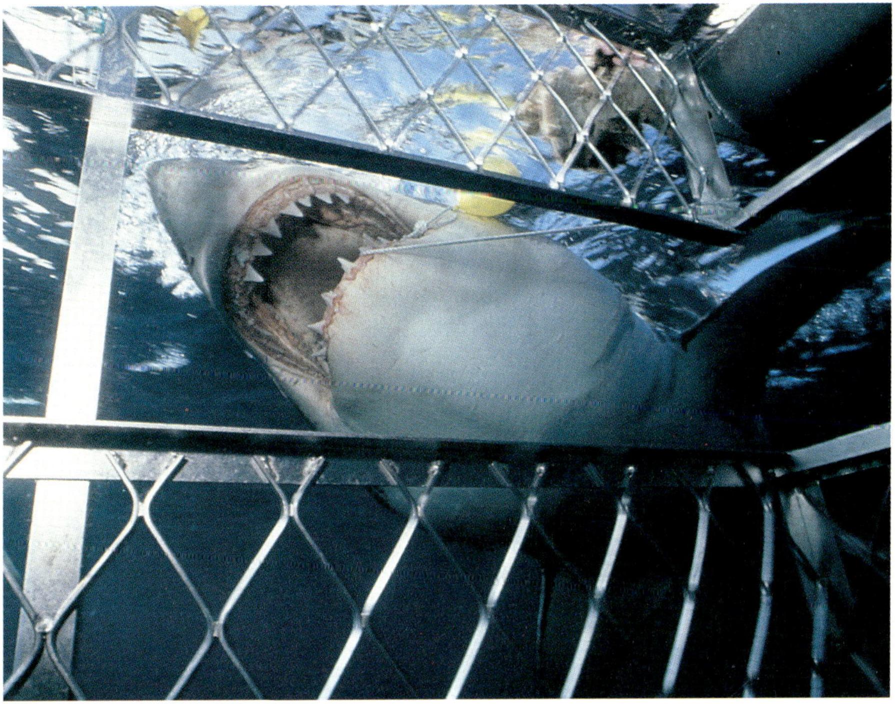

Rourke Book Co., Inc.
Vero Beach, Florida 32964

Edited by Pamela J.P. Schroeder

PHOTO CREDITS
All photos © Marty Snyderman except p. 8 © Lynn M. Stone

Library of Congress Cataloging-in-Publication Data
Cooper, Jason, 1942-
Great white shark / by Jason Cooper.
p. cm. — (Giants among us)
Includes index.
Summary: Describes the physical characteristics, habitat, and behavior of this powerful, swift predator.
ISBN 1-55916-185-X
1. White shark—Juvenile literature. [1. White shark. 2. Sharks.] I. Title. II. Series: Cooper, Jason, 1942- Giants among us.
QL638.95.L3C66 1997
597.3'3—dc21 96-52098
CIP
AC

Printed in the USA

TABLE OF CONTENTS

GREAT WHITE SHARK

No animal in the sea is feared more than the great white shark. It is a powerful, swift **predator** (PRED a tor), or hunter, and one of the giants of the ocean.

The great white is not the largest **species** (SPEE sheez), or kind, of shark. It is, however, the largest of the "man-eaters." Man-eaters are sharks that sometimes attack and kill people.

The great white's weapons are its big, toothy jaws.

The great white shark is white underneath, but slate-colored on top.

THE WHITE GIANT

The great white shark is smaller than the whale and basking sharks. However, it is still huge. The largest known great white was 29 1/2 feet (9 meters) long. It probably weighed 10,000 pounds (4,540 kilograms), the same as a huge hippo.

The whale shark is the largest fish. It may grow 60 feet (18.3 m) long and weigh 50,000 pounds (22,523 kg). Whale sharks, though, are not dangerous to people or sea **mammals** (MA muhlz). They eat small fish and tiny sea creatures known as **plankton** (PLANK ton).

This great white shark trails the line from a fishing net as it cruises the Pacific Ocean.

WHERE GREAT WHITE SHARKS LIVE

Great white sharks live in nearly every ocean. They are most often found in **temperate** (TEM per it) oceans. Temperate water is not too hot and not too cold.

Great white sharks often lurk in the seas around seal **colonies** (KAHL un neez). Seals are a favorite **prey** (PRAY), or food, of great whites.

Many great whites swim near the seal colonies at Año Nuevo Island, California.

Safe on sand, these elephant seals at Año Nuevo, California, won't be as safe when they return to the sea, where great white sharks swim.

PUPS, THE BABY SHARKS

Great white shark pups begin a life of killing before they are born! A mother great white holds several eggs in her body. They hatch inside her, but at different times. As a new shark pup hatches, it becomes prey for an older, stronger brother or sister. Only the last two pups alive are born.

This great white shark survived by eating its brothers and sisters before it was born!

The whale shark is the world's largest

fish, but harmless to the diver.

PREDATOR AND PREY

A great white shark usually hunts living prey, such as seals, fish, and sea turtles. Sometimes it feeds upon large dead animals.

The great white's longest teeth are 3 inches (7.7 centimeters). The teeth are sharp, saw-edged, and deadly. With one bite, a 16-foot (5-m) great white can tear a 30-pound (14-kg) piece of meat from a dead whale.

An adult great white shark has no enemies, except people.

The great white shark's tooth (white) looks small next to those of its ancient relative, the megalodon *shark.*

GREAT WHITE SHARK HABITS

Scientists know little about the private lives of great white sharks. When, where, and why they travel are some of the mysteries.

Great whites' age is a mystery, too, but scientists think that they can live to be at least 35 years old.

Scientists know that great whites have good vision and keen hearing. They can sense even tiny movements in the sea.

The shark's sense of smell is extremely sharp. It helps the shark find prey, even in deep, dark water.

This great white shark smelled the fisherman's bait long before it saw the bait.

GREAT WHITE SHARK COUSINS

Scientists know of more than 350 species of sharks. The great white belongs to a group of sharks called mackerel sharks.

The mackerel species all have the sharp snout and long, streamlined body of the great white. None, however, is anywhere near as big.

Like the great white, several mackerel sharks are game fish. The shortfin mako is a popular game fish and food fish.

The shortfin mako shark, a cousin of the great white, is one of the fastest fish in the sea. It is a popular food and game fish.

PEOPLE AND GREAT WHITE SHARKS

Seeing great white sharks is a thrill for divers in steel cages. Catching great whites is a thrill for sport fishermen.

Unfortunately, great white sharks are most famous for their rare attacks on people. That fame is due partly to *Jaws,* a very popular book and movie.

Jaws is a make-believe story. It tells about a huge great white shark that liked to attack people and their boats.

In real life, sharks of all kinds kill fewer than 100 people each year. Often, no one knows what kind of shark attacked.

A diver bravely photographs a great white shark.

SAVING GREAT WHITE SHARKS

Fishermen and fishing boat nets catch thousands of great white sharks each year. Scientists think that the number of great whites around the world is growing smaller. Some day, great white sharks could be quite rare.

Great white sharks are important to the life of the sea. Like other big predators, they often kill sick or injured prey. Sharks help keep groups of prey animals healthy.

Glossary

colony (KAHL uh nee) — a group of animals of the same kind living together

mammal (MA muhl) — animals that produce milk for their young, and have fur or hair

plankton (PLANK ton) — tiny, floating plants and animals of the sea and other bodies of water

predator (PRED a tor) — an animal that hunts other animals for food

prey (PRAY) — an animal that is hunted by another animal for food

species (SPEE sheez) — within a group of closely-related animals, one certain kind, such as a *whale* shark

temperate (TEM per it) — refers to places and temperatures that are not too hot and not too cold

INDEX